Who Wants To BeA Millionaire?

Life Lessons Learned

LaVone C. Hicks

DEDICATION

This book is dedicated to my loving family: Carter, my husband of 34 years; my three sons LeDarius, DeMarcus, and JeCari; my sisters Pat and Juanita; and my grandchildren who I love to life; Gregory, Kelis, and Dariyus. Thanks for not "clipping my wings" as I began to soar. To Nate Bell and Christian Poulsen who gave me my start and were instrumental in training a "greenie" about finances. And last but not least, to my pastor, Apostle Norbert E. Simmons, who ignited the entrepreneurial spirit in me, helped me to stay grounded in the Word of God, and always leads by example.

CONTENTS

Acknowledgments   i

1 **LIVE "BENEATH" YOUR MEANS**   3

2 **THE TIME VALUE OF MONEY**   7

3 **PLAN FOR LIVING AND LEAVING**   13

4 **WHERE DO YOU FIT IN THE PICTURE?**   17

5 **OTHER TIPS FOR SAVING MONEY**   20

6 **SUMMARY**   22

7 **ABOUT THE AUTHOR**   24

PREFACE

This book is not for those who live on easy street and have their financial act together. But rather for those who live paycheck to paycheck and seem to stay in a rut. It is a self-help guide that is jam packed with information that will guide them to save money, reduce debt, and reach a successful retirement. Told from my perspective as both an insurance agent and a consumer, it is my prayer that they will find these tools so easy to understand, that with commitment and focus, they too will end up on easy street.

1 LIVE "BENEATH" YOUR MEANS

Take a look at the situation in America today. Though the average lifespan is increasing, most people do not have enough in retirement and some have no retirement at all. So you may say, "How can I save for retirement if I don't even have enough to pay my bills?" Well, rather than live *within* your means, you should live *beneath* your means if you want a better financial future. It starts with having a budget. No matter what you earn, you need some parameters by which to go. Here is the monthly budget that I suggest:

Savings – (after tithing 10%, pay yourself 10%)- 20%

Housing (mortgage or rent) – 30%

Transportation- 15%

Debt – (credit cards, loans, etc.) – 15%

Other (food, clothing, entertainment, etc) 20%

If you want to keep the curses off you, and the windows of heaven to open for you, I highly suggest you tithe your ten per cent on the **gross**, the amount on the check before all the taxes and other deductions are taken out. However, for demonstration purposes only, I am using the take home monthly pay of $1000 dollars. That would mean tithing is $100. Next you pay yourself ten per cent of $1000 which also is $100. This brings you to a total of **20%** for savings. Notice that the savings is listed first. That's because if you try to take it out after you've paid all other bills, it just won't be there. It's important to *make saving a priority*.

Next would be $300 for housing if we figured 30% of $1000. You may have to get a roommate to make this work but I'm trying to keep it real. This is what some people take home. Just tell yourself, "This is only temporary. If I make sacrifices now, I'll reap the benefits later." Sometimes renting may be a better choice due to the responsibilities of paying for insurance, maintenance, and property taxes on a home.

In order to get to a job you need transportation. Allocate 15% towards this area, or in this case $150. This may mean walking, carpooling, taking the bus, or driving an old used car, but stay focused. This won't last forever.

The next one is debt. Here is where most people have gotten into deep trouble and for many reasons. Many have not had parents who knew how to teach them about money because they just barely made it themselves. Out of ignorance, wrong choices were made that caused Americans to become laden with debt early on. Slick sales people did not take into account the overall debt when that car or house was sold. And the cost of insurance and medical costs are shocking. And let's not forget what I call the "microwave" generation who just has to have it right now. So to find out that 15% of the take home pay should be our standard is a little surprising. In this case no more than $150 should go towards debt and that includes credit cards, store cards, and personal loans. If you want to put more in this category you'll have to take from somewhere else. Many adults have lived with their parents until they could get on their feet, which is understandable. But always have a plan of exit.

The last category is the one into which everything else falls, simply called "other". This 20%, or $200 in our example, takes care of food, clothing, entertainment, etc.

Of course, the more you make the more you can put into these categories, but everyone needs a budget. If I had known these rules when I began teaching 34 years ago, I could have been a millionaire on the same income. **It's not just how much you make, but how much you save and how you do it.**

One memorable time of saving is when my boys were living at home and we canceled our cable. I thought they, along with my husband, would die at first. But we soon found out that we still had some good entertainment on the local channels. "A penny saved is a penny earned".

Isn't it amazing how quickly one can get into debt, but how long it takes to get out of it? You could charge $3000 to a credit card, but if you made the minimum payments of $15 a month, it would take 39 years to pay it off at a 19.8% interest rate and $10,000 in interest. Simply amazing!

There are several schools of thought on methods to eliminate debt. For many years I supported the high to low interest rate plan where you channeled all extra money to the bill with the highest interest rate first. I like the one that Dave Ramsey (author and radio/TV host) and others call the *debt snowball* method better because the feeling of accomplishment comes sooner.

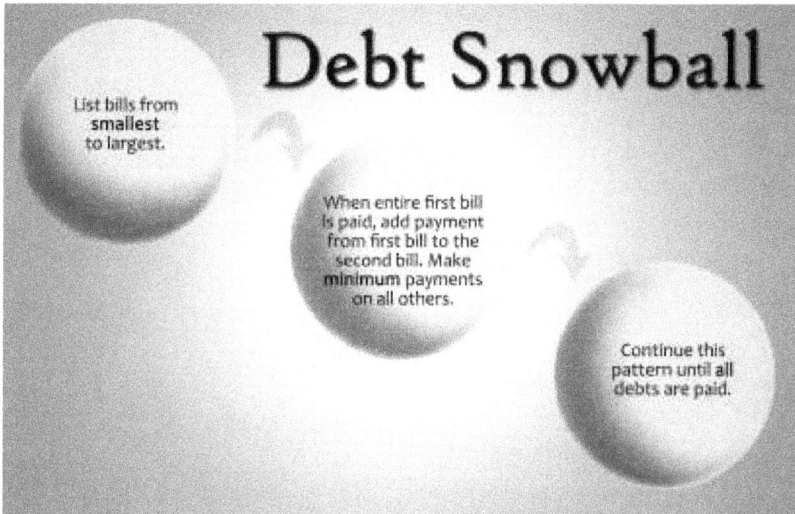

The strategy is very simple. List your bills from the smallest to the largest. Apply any extra money to the smallest bill while making minimum payments on all others. When bill number one is paid off, add that payment to the payment of the second bill until it's paid off. This increase will quickly get that bill paid off too. Continue this pattern with the third bill and so on until all bills are paid. Most people can be debt free in less than 10 years, including the mortgage! Remember, to stay focused though. It gets very tempting to get a hot, new car or nice furniture, etc. *But the debt free ending will justify the sacrificial means.*

2 THE TIME VALUE OF MONEY

Understanding how money works is important to planning savings strategies. Planning for retirement begins when you start working. (Again, I wish someone had put their foot down and demanded that I do it). The "Time Value" of money rewards those who begin saving early. Listen to this example: Mary, who was 30 years old, began saving $5000 a year. After ten years, she stopped contributing but let it stay in the plan. Her twin, Bill, began saving $5000 a year at age 40 and continued for 15 years. Who do you think had the most at retirement? It was Mary. She had the power of compounding on her side. Let's show you the **rule of 72.**

	3%	6%	12%
20	$2,000	$2,000	$2,000
26			$4,000
32		$4,000	$8,000
38			$16,000
44	$4,000	$8,000	$32,000
50			$64,000
56		$16,000	$128,000
62			$256,000
68	$8,000	$32,000	$512,000

This mathematical formula says divide the interest rate you're getting into the number 72 to find out how many years it takes for your money to double. The easiest example would be to take current bank checking account rates which are less than 1%. 1 goes into 72, 72 times. So it takes **72 years for $1000 to double to $2000.**

So in the chart on p.7, you see $2000 saved at age 20, but at three different interest rates. At 3% the money doubles every 24 years (3 goes into 72 twenty-four times) so that at age 68 it has doubled twice to make $8000. At 6% it doubles every 12 years to make $32,000 at age 68. At 12% interest rate, the money doubles every 6 years. This short period allows the money to double eight times before age 68 resulting in a whopping **$512,000!** Isn't that astounding? Nothing is different except the interest rate. So it pays to save early and to get as high an interest rate as possible. ***Work smarter, not harder!***

I remember years ago when my children were young my mother, Jessie Bell Coley, who was diabetic and on dialysis, applied for SSI (Supplemental Security Income) for assistance and was declined. My sister and I took turns driving her the 40 and sometimes 60 miles for her four hour dialysis treatments. After she died, a lady called from social services to inform us that because our mother should have received financial help and had been wrongly denied, we would each get a check. We shouted. We cried. I don't know what I did with my share, but if I had known the rule of 72 and saved just half, I would be sitting much prettier now.

You need a strategy to save or you will miss out on thousands of potential dollars. The three basic ways to save are as follows: Look at this wedding cake design to understand the order of importance.

"Three Tiers of Savings"

Rainy Day Fund

There for medical emergencies, car repairs, credit card avoidance. It needs to be readily available. A savings or money market account w/ check writing privileges is recommended, not just your everyday checking account.

Big- Ticket Fund

This short- term savings is for the big item you plan to purchase within about five years. It might be a house down payment, a college fund, living expenses. It could be ear-marked for a new roof, a new car, or even a major vacation. CD's, short- term bonds, or online savings accounts can be used for these predictable expenses, but not until the proper time.

Long- Term Savings

The goal for these funds is to allow your money to grow. Ideally, it will eventually be the biggest piece of your cake, broad enough to support a long and active retirement. A diversified portfolio is ideal for this goal. Being at the bottom of the cake, it is the least accessible. It's recommended that you leave it alone until the proper time has come, otherwise, your cake might crumble. Examples of products for this purpose are IRAs, 401-K's and annuities.

Rainy Day Fund
Should be "liquid assets", which means funds are accessed easily with no cost to retrieve them. Little interest available on these products.

Big- Ticket Fund
A little hassle may be involved to retrieve these funds in exchange for higher interest.

Long- Term Savings
Rules, tax regulations, and penalties may be associated with early withdrawal in exchange for possibility of higher earnings in the long run. It's recommended that you see a tax accountant.

Your rainy day fund is your emergency fund. Having this money will keep you from having to use credit cards or get loans in emergencies or borrow from your retirement. The money needs to be in a place where you can easily access the funds so don't expect to get much interest. A bank savings account or money market account would work fine for this. Try to accumulate at least $500-$1000 here before you start to work on big ticket fund. The big ticket money could be placed somewhere that gives a little more interest like a certificate of deposit (CD) or internet banks such as ally.com or HSBCdirect.com You'll get a slightly higher interest rate. I would still put a minimal amount in retirement while I'm putting the most in the rainy day and the big ticket accounts until they're funded. Then I'd step up the retirement even more. (This is the 10% savings we discussed in chapter 1).

For retirement, there are several options: The most common is the 401(k) plan that you may receive on your job. It is tax deferred meaning the interest that's earned is not taxed until you withdraw it. Unless your employer is contributing, however, you may as well invest in a Roth individual retirement account (IRA). This way, the money you contribute has already been taxed and after five years you can access the principle if needed for things like a house down payment. These plans have rules and regulations and you should seek professional help when implementing them. They must be withdrawn by age 70 1/2. Because the money is in the stock market you have the potential to earn more interest, but the there is also the potential for loss.

Because of the volatility of the stock market, another retirement product is getting lots of attention these days. It is the *equity indexed annuity*. It is an insurance product that is linked to the performance of an index such as the S&P 500, yet protects your principal when the index declines. It solves the following concerns for those nearing retirement:

1. Ensures continued growth of assets (because of inflation)
2. Generates lifetime income
3. Protects savings while withdrawing
4. Minimizes taxes (Taxes taken as withdrawn like a 401(k))
5. Provides double the money if skilled nursing is needed. (Some)
6. Leaves a legacy for heirs

Let me share a few facts from the US Census Bureau to help you see the importance of strategizing for retirement early:

- The average American lives to be 78.7 years
- By 2025, 62 million are expected to be over 65
- Those age 85 will double by 2030 and 20% of the population will be drawing social security
- 2/3 of all retirees rely on social security for half their income
- 30 million people age 55 are in the workforce because they can't afford to retire and still need health insurance.
- People will spend more years in retirement and have less support from traditional plans such as social security and defined benefit plans as those offered by the state.

There are two methods to determine the amount of income needed in retirement:

1. Replacement ratio (60% of annual current income)
2. Projected expense method (Itemize living expenses)

One important note: according to the *Trinity Study*, a portfolio's ability to provide lifetime income depends in large part on the withdrawal rate used (usually 4-5%).

What does all this mean? *We must rely on personal assets and wisdom to meet our financial needs in retirement. The only thing worse than death is outliving your money.*

In order to keep someone else from making this mistake, I'm going to share with you the biggest financial mistake I've ever made. About five years after being in the financial services business part-time, I was so hyped up until I decided to leave teaching and go fulltime in insurance by opening an office. Upon finding out that once separated from the state my retirement money was available to me, out of ignorance *I withdrew my retirement.* Not only did I pay the penalty for withdrawing before age 59 1/2, but I also had to pay taxes on the money. So the government got about 1/3 of the total amount. Remember the time value of money? Had it remained where it was, the return with the state retirement was around 6%. Divide 6 into 72. So the money would double about every twelve years which would mean right now it could be working towards doubling again. I returned to teaching the next year realizing that I missed the kids, I needed the steady income, but most of all I needed the health benefits. So if you get a pink slip or leave a job that has retirement, leave it there, roll it over into an IRA or an equity indexed annuity. But by all means, **don't cash in your retirement**. You can't get the years back unless you pay the money back.

3 PLAN FOR LIVING AND LEAVING

Not only can insurance products help in retirement and leave a legacy, but they can also take care of final expenses. One should prepare for longevity with adequate retirement money and prepare for death with adequate life insurance.

The purpose of life insurance is to ensure financial security of the family in case of premature death, preserve estates and pay fees, meet final expenses, clear outstanding debt, and support favorite charities.

There are really only two types of life insurance: **Whole life** (permanent), and **term life**. They may be given different names depending on lots of moving parts such as fixed or flexible *benefits*, *accrual of cash value* which may be fixed or flexible, and the *premium amount* which may be fixed or flexible. Take a look at the following definitions:

- **Term life-** like a "lease". Lasts for a certain amount of time, then it's over. Affordable and requires medical investigation. Can be declined for health reasons. No cash value. May be renewed from one to thirty years.

- **Whole Life-** Builds cash value.

   Some require an exam. Others do not.

   Some are guaranteed issue.

   Cost more than term.

Other names: *Adjustable premium, flexible premium, universal life, variable universal life, and indexed universal life.*

There is no "One size fits all" type of life insurance. For example, a single person with no debt or children just needs enough for final expenses. (According to NFDA 2013 general price list, the average funeral cost $8,343 and rising. See www.funeral.org) The following factors help a good agent to determine the best product:

1. Age
2. Health including height and weight
3. Debt and mortgage
4. Number of children
5. Amount of income

"Old School" agents use an acronym called the D-I-M-E theory.

D- Death and debt
I - Income. About 10x annual salary
M- Mortgage balance
E- Education. Around 50k per child

Based on the DIME theory, a 40 year old male home owner in good health making $40,000 per year with three children would easily need over $500,000 in coverage. Since whole life costs about 3 xs more than term, a 30 year term would be a better suit for him costing around $50 per month. (By the way, if you have a family and are spending more than the15% on a late model vehicle and don't have life insurance, you just traded your family's security for a car. As a Christian, I believe you should put **God *first, then people, then things.***

On the other hand, a 50 year old female homeowner, in good health, who has an empty nest, could change to a permanent whole life policy. A universal life policy builds cash value and could be borrowed from in an emergency. A 100,000 dollar benefit would cost her around $50 a month. However, if she's had recent cancer, or has diabetes along with high blood pressure and cholesterol issues, she may only qualify for a final expense whole life product which has a minimal death benefit from 5k to 50k depending on the age and health status. No medical exam is required. They do build cash value and may be borrowed against in emergencies. But if the loan isn't paid back, it will come off the death benefit when insured dies, with interest. Please note too, if you don't borrow from the cash value, it goes to the insurance company at insureds death. The best thing to do, if you can't repay the loan, is to pay the interest on the loan each year. Life insurance should be reviewed about every five years or when a life change is triggered.

*Now that our kids are grown and gone, we have changed our life insurance for the last time. We kept a little term, but to beef up our retirement, we chose an **indexed universal life** permanent product, while we're still healthy, to take us to the finish line. Not only is it permanent insurance, but it can act as a retirement or extra emergency fund because we can add more money to the premium amount. For example, if the premium were $100 per month, we could increase it to say $140. We could also send a lump sum amount. (We have to ask the company what our contribution limits are to keep from triggering a taxable event). If we are running short one month, we can skip a payment. The cash value builds annually because it's linked to the S & P 500, a Standard and Poors index, which historically has averaged nearly 10%. Unlike a final expense whole life, any amount borrowed does not have to be paid back and is withdrawn **tax free.** That's because the interest on the loan is low, something like 2%, and the interest earned historically outpaces it by nearly 7%. Now we have 401(k)'s, annuities, life insurance, and our job's defined benefit retirement plan to depend on.*

These safety nets are in place to keep us from depending on social security, which was never meant to be a primary source for retirement. Social security replaces less than 40% for wage earners age 65 and declines to 29% by 2030, so don't count on it. If you take early retirement at age 62, you lose 7% of the full retirement amount for the rest of your life. So try to hang in there, unless you have health issues and can't work or have some dire financial need. (I did discover that a spouse can take 50% of the older spouses' social security, if he/she is still working. Then stop and claim their own full retirement, when of age, without affecting the older spouses retirement) Check the rules on this issue out at www.ssa.gov.

Since this chapter is mainly about insurance, have you ever heard of the *FTC Funeral Rule*? The Federal Trade Commission is the nation's consumer protection agency who works to prevent fraud and deceptive practices in the marketplace. The Funeral Rule, enforced by the FTC, says you have the right to buy separate goods (such as caskets) and services (such as embalming or a memorial service). You don't have to accept a package that includes things you don't want. Funeral directors must give you a price over the phone if you ask for it and you don't have to give them your name. You don't even have to buy the casket or urn from them! If you bought it online or at a local casket store or somewhere else, they can't refuse. You can read about these points and much more at: www.consumer.ftc.gov/articles/0300-ftc-funeral-rule.

4 WHERE DO YOU FIT IN THE PICTURE?

If you are age 49 and below, you are in a better position to improve your financial future. Use the chart below to insert your own take home pay in each first line to get what goes in each second line. You will know exactly what you should be spending in each category.

YOUR PERSONAL BUDGET

.10x gross   = _____   Tithes *

.10x take home = _____   Savings

.30 x _____ = _____   Housing

.15x _____   = _____   Transport

.15x _____   = _____   Consumer debt

.25 x _____ = _____   Other

*A non-tither can place this 10% in any other area.

In addition to setting up the budget as described in chapter one, here are some other suggestions to make sure you have in place:

- Pay bills on time (reduce short term debts, 2 credit cards)
- Build savings (bank savings acct., money market, online banks, CDs, Retirement Account)
- Get Insurance (medical, disability, life, car, home)
- Clear errors on credit report
- Obtain credit score (work to get 720 or higher)

In my child-bearing years, I did not have disability insurance. I remember bringing home $500 a month in the 1980s. Little did I know that having a disability policy would have triggered extra income when I had my children. Well it's too late for that now, but I'm ready for any future ailment.

If you are age 50 and up, just know this: "Your health is your wealth". Healthcare is one of the largest expenses in retirement. A year's stay in a **private nursing facility** currently costs an average of **$84,000**, or $230 per day, and this figure continues to rise. Here are current median costs for various types and levels of care as reported in the *Genworth Cost of Care Survey: Home Care Providers, Assisted Living Facilities and Nursing Homes* as of 2013. **Homemaker services-$18** hourly rate (housekeeping, cooking, etc). **Home health aid services- $19 per hr** (assists with ADL's like feeding, bathing, transferring, etc). **Adult Day Care- $65 per day** (support services in a community setting). **Assisted living facilities- $41,400 per year** for a private one-bedroom. So if you're like me, force yourself to eat right and exercise. You have less time to prepare yourself. But as the old adage goes, "Better late than never." Here are the keys to have in place or to get in place as quickly as possible:

- Get long term care insurance while you're healthy and premiums will be lower. 70% of Americans over 65 will need it. Medicare only pays for skilled care in nursing homes. After 100 days, you're on your own. To get Medicaid you have to spend down most assets. With LTC you get to choose your type of care and protect your assets. *I visited a retired colleague in Charlotte, NC recently. She told me that when she was working at Duke she purchased a long term care policy. Now that she's retired, she's still paying $30* *per month. Premiums don't change as you age. Not everyone in a nursing home is old. Some have injuries or chronic diseases.*

- Pay off long term debts like cars and homes.
- Review investment portfolios. You can't afford to lose money now.
- Focus on estate planning and wills.
- Review or adjust life insurance policies.
- Join AARP. Member Advantages offer Finder mobile app lets you locate and map places that offer their discounts on the go. Download app from ITunes or the google app store.

*Important note: Medicare does not cover prescriptions. If you leave your group health plan when you go on Medicare, you are responsible for *selecting a prescription plan from a private company.* Don't wait until you need an expensive medicine to find a RX plan. If you do, you'll have to wait until the next AEP (annual enrollment period) and you will be penalized 1% of the national monthly average of the premium for every month you could have had it, but didn't. This cost will be added to your monthly premium for as long as you have a prescription plan. CMS, Center for Medicare and Medicaid Services, will not accept your not knowing as an excuse. Now you know. (See medicare.gov)

5 OTHER TIPS FOR SAVING MONEY

- Use a broker for auto and life insurance. They can search and find the best value for your money by representing several companies. (*I recently had my broker check for me, and am now saving $30 per month for the same services*)
- Use www.mint.com on your phone or computer to help you budget.
- Increase your deductible (the amount you pay before the insurance company pays) on your car and home to receive an immediate reduction in premium. (This is only if you'd rather pay out of pocket rather than risk your premiums going up if you were to file a claim).
- Ask credit card and mortgage companies for a lower rate (If you've paid on time they'd rather negotiate than see you leave. Banks can do an "in house modification" and won't require an appraisal or upfront fees) *I've had a modification on my mortgage twice since I've been a homeowner. It saved me about $150 per month.*
- Ask about the "equal payment plan" with your electric company. They look at the total for your last 12 months. Divide by 12 to give you an equal amount for the next 12 months. This helps with budgeting.
- Buy in bulk from *Sam's* or *Costco*. Basic things like paper towels, toilet tissue, and toothpaste are much cheaper.
- Pay bills automatically. Individual companies offer this service or you can set bill payments up through your bank. This method saves time, stamps, and increases your credit score by paying on time.
- Use local credit unions. They have lower fees and are in business to help their members. If you can't join one, *Woodforest National Banks* are located in many Walmart stores and will allow checking accounts to be

opened with as little as $10.00.

- Buy school clothes on clearance in July and winter clothes on clearance in January.
- Get free eyeglasses online at www.coastal.com. You will need your prescription for your eyes and an email address. At checkout, enter code "firstpairfree".
- Free credit report at www.annualcreditreport.com
- Free credit score at www.creditkarma.com
- Compare credit card rates at www.bankrate.com
- Nagging creditors? Tired of telemarketers calling? Register your phone number at www.donotcall.gov
- Be money smart. Visit www.knowdebt.org/education,
- www.feedthepig.org, www.econedlink.org, www.jumpstart.com, www.choosetosave.com. www.daveramsey.com, suzeorman.com, and cheapskatemonthly.com for financial literacy.
- Buy and sell on craigslist or eBay
- Use www.retailmenot.com or www.ratherbeshopping.com to save on purchases.
- Save on airplane tickets by shopping airfarewatchdog.com, farecompare.com, or yapta.com.
- Dial 1(800)free411 for information services
- Comparison shop at these websites: shopzilla, pricegrabber, sortprice, couponmom, couponcabin, and edeals.com.
- Invest at treasurydirect.com (TIPS- treasury inflation protected securities)
- Computershare.com
- Sharebuilder.com
- Oneshare.com

SUMMARY

To wrap it all up, you should budget, reduce debt, strategize your savings, spend less on necessities by comparison shopping, and invest properly and early. Remember, ***increased longevity coupled with spiraling medical cost can jeopardize even the best planned retirement.***

When I first came into the financial services business all "bright-eyed and bushy-tailed", my goal was to be a multi-millionaire by age 45. As time went on, I began to realize that wealth and happiness were not synonymous. This fact has been highlighted in recent years by the sheer number of well-to-do people who are committing suicide, the rising divorce rate, and threat of war around the world.

Because I have God in my life, my health, my home, a wonderful job as a teacher, another job as a financial educator and insurance agent, and a loving family, I've concluded that I'm rich beyond measure. My financial goal is not so much to be a millionaire, as it is to be removed of any weights that would hinder me from doing His will. But the fact is, as I tell my adult sons and groups to which I speak, you *will never be wealthy working for someone else.* With a system in our country that rewards those at the top and neglects those underneath, you'll never get paid what you're worth.

So what's the answer? It's two-fold. In the economic climate in which we live today, one needs to know how to do more than one thing in case of job loss. So find a profession that you love to do and you'll never dread going to work. (For me it has been music). Ask God to help you discover your purpose, and then make a business out of it. (I never thought I would have a passion for finances, but God made my misery become my ministry and equipped me to serve on a broader basis.) Now you're in control of your income and there is no limit to how far you can go. Beyond that, other non-tangibles have given me great wealth. To take a paragraph from the *Daily Wealth Confession:*

I call my house and all of my property paid in full. I believe I receive raises and bonuses; sales and commissions; favorable settlements; estates and inheritances; interest and income; rebates and returns; discounts and dividends; checks in the mail; gifts and surprises; lost money found; bills paid off; blessings and income. Thank you Lord for giving me the power to create wealth so that I have more than enough to give unto Your Kingdom. ***Money cometh to me now!! You are bringing me into my wealthy place!!!***

-***How to Find Your Wealthy Place,*** Dr. Leroy Thompson, Sr.

About the Author....

LaVone Coley Hicks, Owner, President and CEO of *Hicks & Associates Insurance & Financial Services*, does not have your typical financial background. In fact, she is a nationally recognized music teacher who has shared her passion for music with her students in NC for over 33 years. Residing in Goldsboro, she has a Bachelor of Arts degree from Johnson C. Smith University, Charlotte, N. C., and a Masters in Education from the University of North Carolina, Charlotte, N.C. Her nearly two decades of experience in insurance and financial services was acquired through a myriad of trials with money early on that motivated her to seek knowledge to overcome them.

This journey began when Mrs. Hicks became licensed in 1996 so she could share information with others. After serving as Regional Leader with *Primerica Financial Services* for seven years, she joined *Capitalchoice Financial Services* in 2003 and quickly became a Regional Marketing Director and later joined *Federal Financial Group, LLC.* She is enjoying being an independent agent and offers several workshops which include: *Exiting with Excellence; Teen MoneyTalk; Economic Keys to Success; 21st Century Health Trends; Health, Wealth and Wisdom; Financial Fitness Workshop; Your Medicare Options,* and *Who Wants To Be A Millionaire.*

 LaVone Hicks continues on a mission with integrity to dispel ignorance and empower others through sharing sound principles in accessing life, health, long term care, annuities, and Medicare insurance as well as advocating financial literacy.

www.ingramcontent.com/pod-product-compliance
Lightning Source LLC
Chambersburg PA
CBHW070749210326
41520CB00016B/4650